Just Be Me

Dedicated to my daughter – my little but strong lioness. You love and you roar. Just be you!

TOSARI THOMAS

Copyright © 2024 Tosari Thomas

Illustrations by Magic Media, CANVA

ISBN: 978-1-7637936-1-3

Independently published

All rights reserved. No part of this publication may be reproduced or transmitted in any form or by any means without the prior written permission of the author.

Mummy elephant keeps her youngest calf on the inside of the group, as they stomp and travel together in the wild.

Mummy kangaroo keeps her joey in her warm pouch, skin on skin and nestled in.

As the little one grows inside Mummy dolphin, she whistles a song so her calf will know her mummy's sound.

Mummy panda gently cradles her young cub, until she can move about and explore on her own.

A few days before her tiny piglets are born, Mummy pig scurries around to make them a home, a cosy, leafy nest.

Brave mummy cheetah keeps her litter safe and sound, by moving to new places where they can run and play without worry.

Young calf won't sleep for the first few weeks, so Mummy whale will patiently keep watch and stay awake too.

Mummy lioness and cub play fight, they pounce and bounce, as she teaches her how to defend her pride.

Mother hen makes sure her chicks are always well-fed as they peck at tasty seeds and grains.

When the little cub slowly opens its eyes to the world, Mummy polar bear is ready with lots of milk and comfort.

Just like the mummy animals, little girls know how to care in their own special way too.

As mummy bear looks after her cubs, little girls take good care of their teddy bears.

And little girls give the best comfort when their baby brother is feeling sad.

Little girls know how to protect others. They dress up as superheroes, small but brave defenders.

Little girls are special from the start. Someday little girls, with big hearts will be the greatest mummies of them all!